D1738876

Do Inhabit

Style your space for a
creative and considered life.

Sue Fan and Danielle Quigley

CHRONICLE BOOKS
SAN FRANCISCO

Library of Congress Cataloging-in-Publication Data

Names: Fan, Sue, author. | Quigley, Danielle, author.
Title: Do inhabit : style your space for a creative and considered life / Sue
  Fan and Danielle Quigley.
Description: San Francisco : Chronicle Books LLC., 2019. | "First published
  in the United Kingdom in 2018 by The Do Book Company." | Includes
  bibliographical references.
Identifiers: LCCN 2018047260 | ISBN 9781452180274 (pb : alk. paper)
Subjects: LCSH: Interior decoration—Psychological aspects.
Classification: LCC NK2113 .F36 2019 | DDC 747—dc23 LC record available at
https://lccn.loc.gov/2018047260

Manufactured in China.

Cover design by James Victore.
Book designed and set by Ratiotype.

10 9 8 7 6 5 4 3 2 1

Chronicle Books LLC
680 Second Street
San Francisco, California 94107
www.chroniclebooks.com

Contents

Prologue

As you walk through your front door and kick off your shoes, you put down your bag on the antique pew bench and your keys in the jute basket, hang up your jacket on the elephant brass hook, and get the sensation you're not going to want to leave.

There's a faint scent of cedar in the air. You glance up and take in the big, bold oil painting centered on the wall, the statement light fixture in the corner throwing off intricate shadows and a warm glow, and the soft, faded-blue Persian rug under your feet, and, little by little, the details of home slowly start to flood your senses.

Piñon logs are stacked in a handmade firewood rack next to the burning woodstove; there is eucalyptus wildly artful in a vintage milk glass vase. Greenery is scattered throughout. Books are stacked by the armchair with blankets over ottomans. There are pops of color on the tables. Stories untold in picture frames and trinkets. Ranges of textures throughout the room, from wall hangings to throw cushions. Everything is thoughtfully placed, beautifully designed.

This is a home that feels lived in and loved. It feels intimate, inviting, interesting, but not overwhelmingly so. Consideration and beauty are apparent in every corner.

Introduction

We love coming home. We love the welcoming nature of thoughtfulness, intention, and, of course, great style. We love having well-worn spots where our shoes, dog leashes, and bags routinely sit. The weight of the day comes off alongside our belongings. We catch a glimpse of a framed photobooth strip hung on the wall, of a lichen-covered stick from a walk last weekend set on the coffee table, of air plants dressing the windowsill. We let familiarity find its way in and feel the wave of reassurance and gratitude for a space we've created that perfectly suits us. We find great comfort in knowing which corner is our favorite to curl up in. A space that is ours, where we feel at ease.

Our space and style are an extension of who we are. You can learn so much about a person when you walk into their home. You see character, personality, and practicality intertwine. We are intricately tied to the spaces we inhabit. They affect us—and those around us. They change how we move through our everyday life. Styling a space begins with how we want to live in it and, in essence, how we want to live.

Home is where we put down roots and connect—to ourselves and our families, partners, even our animals. It is a space to rejuvenate and grow. A shelter for what and who we love. A place for our collections—the objects we pick up along the way that weave a tapestry of our stories and memories. Surrounding yourself with things that bring you joy, and that ground you, creates a sense and a space that invite serenity and awareness. We must make space for our senses to come alive—and come to rest. Addresses change and tastes evolve, but our homes should always be a sanctuary.

You may live in a barn, a cabin, a city apartment, or even a boat. There is no size restriction to how a space can feel. Creativity and attention don't end with your personal space, but it's a good place to start. Create a space that contains the things you need to think more freely and express yourself openly. Where you can relax, meditate, entertain, read, and work. Well-being starts where you sleep, eat, and live. This is our guide to help you create such a place.

Less noise, more Earth; less house, more home.

Our Story

We are two friends who have similar tastes, but our personalities are quite different. What we do share is a deep love for beautiful, thoughtful, wild, and intentional things and the stories behind them.

Our story began where these elements all came together. We were photographers by trade and we met in Antarctica fifteen years ago, where we found a shared love for expansive landscapes, natural wonders, and handmade treasures . . . many of the same elements we love now. We continue to incorporate these into our style, work, and daily lives. Traveling to the end of the world is not for the faint of heart. We camped on glaciers, sailed through the Drake Passage, and watched icebergs break apart thunderously and roll into the sea from Zodiac boats. In the moments between the magic and adventure, we found ourselves dreaming of a life filled with the kind of delight beauty brings. By traipsing through this wild continent and through small towns in Argentina and Uruguay, we collected pieces of this Earth that make it whole to us: food from farmers, unique small pebbles, artisan stoneware, paper goods, local music.

Our life and work revolve around making spaces and things beautiful and unique and wild. It is an insatiable pursuit for creating tangible beauty from wilderness. We created Wild Habit—a lifestyle brand and design business—to embrace the essence of who we are and who we strive to be. We are endlessly inspired by nature and all her seasons. We love finding ways to design products and spaces that reflect that. We truly believe a dried poppy pod in the winter is as stunning as in summer's full bloom. We hope to inspire others to see Earth's beauty and care for it. We pair sustainability with handmade wares, styling, and jewelry. We plant trees with proceeds because we believe life is a delicate balance of give and take. We now style for the Do Lectures every summer in Wales and in California. Creating spaces that encompass the elements we love is our dream job. It is our greatest labor of love. We consider every detail.

Prutsen

When it comes to interior design, we have a favorite foreign word: *prutsen*. This Dutch word translates loosely to doing something of very little significance that only looks like work, or tinkering. Only to us, it's quite significant—not the kind of significance that changes the world, but the kind that changes ours (and hopefully yours) and how we feel in it. It's a surprisingly useful way to clear our heads. Little bits of rearranging, picking up wild pieces on dog walks and putting them in vases or bowls, *prutsen* the details because it makes our hearts warm and gets our creative juices flowing. It's unbelievable how much time we can spend placing things here or there. You can sneak it in while the children are napping or make a day of it after a long week of tedious work. The fun in *prutsen* is the spontaneity of it. Instead of defining your style in one fell swoop, you can let it build. Open your eyes to details and consideration and let it feel like play. It will remind you that all details matter and, at the same time, aren't that big of a deal. It's about finding a new place for a houseplant in bloom, making room for a piece of art from a local craft market, or getting around to organizing your bookshelves. *Prutsen* at its finest is simple and fulfilling.

In the end, the details are what will make your house a home—and we've included a whole chapter on the subject. Stories you tell with your art, images, and collections. The natural elements you discover along the way that make you pay attention to your surroundings. Finding your style doesn't come in a box.

Do Inhabit is written as a guide to help you create a space that is considered and even inspires creativity. Somewhere you want to start and end your day. We will share some basic rules and guidelines. We will help you incorporate the things you love into your space. It will be up to you to determine how your space looks. We hope we can help you define how your space feels.

Remember, no effort that we make to attain something beautiful is ever lost.

Helen Keller

1
Style

There's no how-to road map to style.
It's about self-expression and,
above all, attitude.

Iris Apfel

True style is about finding things you like and putting them on show without letting them define you. Your style should be a reflection of your inner, unflinching self.

It's all too easy to get trapped into curating your space with someone else's personality. We're here to tell you to be yourself—and to help you achieve that even if you're sharing your space with others. Pay attention, unplug, reflect, and discover how your space can—and should—be one that reflects your quirks, your delights, your story, your style.

Our Style

If you stepped into our homes, you'd see a lot of similarities. We both love copper and wood. We love antiques, mid-century modern furniture, vintage kitchenware. We love wild dried flora and found pieces of fauna.

You'd also see a lot of differences. That's the beauty of style. You can like a lot of the same things, and even own a lot of the same things, but have different ways of styling them. No two homes will look exactly alike because no two people are exactly the same.

What we like

DQ: It's not for everybody, but I like stuff. My windowsills are full of treasures, most ledges house something wild and something sparkly, and the walls are constantly in need of patching for the rotation of artwork. I like to try things for a while before I commit to where they are going to go, chairs especially. If I see a shape I love, I don't hesitate to buy it and find a place for it later. Some pieces will stay for years—a branch hanging on the wall, something with a sense of humor in the bathroom, chalkboards by the front door, draped sheepskins—and some will move around several times before being sold to make room for something different. I like to hang my prettiest clothes on the door and have my jewelry on display, to showcase my favorite pieces.

I get so much happiness out of using things for the wrong purpose—a candy dish for dog treats, a cloche on my counter for my constant rotation of baked goods, a chair for an end table, a cigar box for napkins. I'm always on the lookout for specific things that can be used for different purposes—vintage boxes, a telephone table, a bar cart.

I'm constantly adding chairs, then swapping them out. Most surfaces have some sort of accent and wild bit.

I operate on a philosophy that if I see something I like, I'll find a place for it, which means there is a good bit of mixing and matching, contrasting colors and textures. It inevitably finds its way into my style.

SF: As a food and prop stylist, I have a soft spot for vintage cookware, ceramics, useful utensils, tools, and textiles. Each wooden spoon in my vintage crock has a story and a purpose. My favorite cookbooks sit stacked on top of one another. My shelves are lined with glass jars filled with grains, nuts, seeds, flours, and whatever I have fermenting. Each drawer and shelf house their own stories. My cutting boards sit on countertops showing off their gorgeous grain. I love a collection that feeds me.

I travel frequently and move often, so if I'm adding things to my life, I try to find pieces that spark fond memories or are useful. This can be as simple as picking up stones, flattening flowers, or framing postcards—or if I'm buying anything, it's usually a blanket, tea towel, or book. I love wood, brass, copper, pottery, and most things old and farm-y. I like furniture that is versatile—that is, convenient to move, stackable, or foldable (it's such fun to find).

I also love keeping old correspondence. I always make room on a wall or the side of a cabinet or shelf for love letters—from my walks through life and all the amazing people I've met. There's nothing more thoughtful or generous than a handwritten note. In the past, I've had to pack a "go bag" for evacuation due to dangerously close wildfires, and in that bag were letters and cards, plus old photos and some wooden spoons.

Mostly, I love anything that encourages sustainability, usefulness, beauty, compassion, and the wild.

Our Homes

DQ: I remember the first time I walked into Sue Fan's home and it immediately felt just like her. It would have been astonishing had it not been so perfectly fitting. There was incense burning in a beautiful brass dish filled with dried rice by the front door (I went almost immediately and bought the same scent and went hunting for the perfect dish), the room had beautiful photography, and cooking and design books were piled thoughtfully but casually on the floor (plenty to look at when I needed some downtime). There were all kinds of framed art hung in just the right spots, nestled among a manzanita branch and pinned-up postcards (some that were even from me!). Everywhere I looked there was something intriguing or a smart solution (even the pretty vessel she kept her dish scrubbers in—why didn't I think of that before?). Her home is a truthful display of her personality—incredibly intentional yet still casual enough to be inviting; highly stimulating but powerfully calming. This is what good style can do and can be, an accurate reflection of who you are.

I have imitated much of what Sue does in her home and yet it looks completely different. I also have a manzanita branch hanging in my home, but I've got some jewelry draped from its branches. It's amazing to see what has changed and what has stayed the same in all the places she has lived over the years.

SF: Danielle makes everything beautiful. She wants it to encompass life. She'll be the first to show you she's not fastidious, but everything in her life has been carefully selected and is meant to be shared. If you find yourself sitting on her sofa, a pretty bowl filled with nuts and chocolate will appear on the coffee table. Next, there'll be a cocktail in a vintage glass in your hand and the perfect music playing in the background. You'll be comfortable and feel cared for, and there will never be a shortage of well-styled bits to keep your eyes occupied.

There is always something new to look at in her home. It could be a new piece of furniture, artwork, paint color, or tree stumps from a neighbor. She is insatiable in keeping her life a rotating gallery. There's always good humor involved, something alluring and wild, and—unfailingly—plenty of sentiment. The best part about her and her home is that nothing is too precious. Her things have value and are always gorgeous, but her home is meant to be lived in. It's incredibly refreshing.

> If you were born without wings, do nothing to prevent them from growing.
>
> Coco Chanel

Finding someone who inspires you is good. In fact, it's the best. Seek out those people. Spend time with them. Pay attention to what they do and get inspired. See what it is that you like about a space, and honor it by imitating it. Just be sure to add your own twist. Maybe you like the way they use rocks as door stoppers. Or sticks as art. Do that. It can't be the same because you won't find the same rock. Or stick. Or antique glasses. Or shelves. It's one of the many reasons we always encourage incorporating items from nature and going to thrift stores. It's often one of a kind. Find joy in the process and in *prutsen*.

How We Style—The Do Lectures

The Do Lectures is an incredibly inspiring lecture series that takes place on an old farm in Cardigan, West Wales. Each year when we start planning for the Do Lectures, it's difficult not to get overwhelmed by the scale of it. The barns no longer house livestock, but the structures are sound and so is the old chicken shed, now the Do headquarters. The old cow shed is the lecture hall and the old machine hall is where all the meals take place. The old donkey shed is now the Do library and whisky den, and there is a magical space below the full-time home of founders David and Clare Hieatt, which becomes a not-so-secret gin bar. There are two fields that house the attendees and the speakers in either canvas bell tents or tepees. The entire farm sits atop a hill with almost 360-degree views over Cardigan Bay, where you can see right down to the sea and just about every shade of green. It's a bucolic wonderland.

Our job is to make the already beautiful space even more so. Our goal is to help enhance and elevate not only the space itself, but everyone's relationship within it. How we go about styling this annual event for a hundred-plus Doers is how we start almost all of our new projects. The same way we clear a space at home, we do it here: assess the space, determine its assets, and establish what we have to work with. Then we consider what the different spaces are going to be used for and how we can get the most out of them. Every space at Do should inspire ideas, change, and doing.

A lot of magic happens on this farm. The transformation is one that can be hard to grasp or even realize unless you show up a week early. Our two favorite transformations are the food barn and the secret gin bar.

The food barn

The food barn has whitewashed walls, aged cracks, and centuries-old wood beams. There are long wooden tables and bench seats that fill the space. Without extra floor space to utilize, we gravitate toward the walls and beam ceilings. Sitting in such a wild part of Wales, we find ferns and moss and lichen at every turn. The Hieatts and their small team of cooks and gardeners assembled for the event grow a wide variety of flowers, vegetables, and herbs on the grounds. It's our playground. We use old roof slates as centerpieces that hold moss- and lichen-covered sticks and tealights, alongside found stones from the nearby beach, and old English milk bottles as vases for fresh-cut flowers. Fairy lights hang from the walls and our handmade birch pendants hang from the beams. We put cut greenery from the landscape into the cracks of the walls and in all the corners to bring the outside in. Everything provides a sense of place. When we can, we bring in herbs for a little extra olfactory sensory delight. We always work to invoke all five senses. Our hope is to let these natural elements feel as if they have subtly and gracefully slipped in.

With the help of a small but talented team, the food barn is transformed into a beautiful, convivial space. Everyone sits cozily together, the entire space is warmly lit, and the food is made by amazing cooks who ensure that every plate is delicious. There's constant chatter over wine, wild centerpieces, and Halen Môn salt crocks. These meals and this space encourage openness and attentiveness.

The secret gin bar

The secret gin bar starts out as a pretty musty old cellar. It is an unused space most of the year, and so it often takes a good scouring from the amazing Do volunteers before we can start our process. We create a living wall in the wooden diamond-back wine racks and fill it with fresh herbs (see page 26). When you walk in, you're immediately greeted by the delicate scents of rosemary, mint, thyme, and sage. The only lighting is a small hanging pendant and candlelight. It's moody, to say the least. Upwards of fifty candles burn each evening. Music always plays. There are old lush red velvet chairs and a soft green chaise longue. Old Persian rugs dot the cement floors. Vintage glasses, candelabras, and side tables fill the small space.

We try to style the seating how we would style a living room—cozy, inviting, ripe for conversation and sociable drinking. Chairs are spaced for intimacy, with plenty of surfaces for putting down a glass. You can always find delicious gin and conversation flowing here through the wee hours of the morning. It's the perfect curated space for style and sophistication in an old cellar on a farm. There's no more perfect pairing for us.

When we create spaces for sharing, we hope the relationships built there stand as long as these old buildings and are always at least half as wild and beautiful.

———————

Styling Advice

Now that you've got a sense of our personal style, let's look at how we might approach a new space and some practical ways to get started.

Clear a room and assess your wants and needs for that space. What is it that you actually need it for? The basic guidelines that follow can be applied to almost any room. And we'll come to room-by-room styling in the next chapter. Note the obvious. "I know this is my living room. I have a couch and television, a coffee table and floor lamp." But then think about how you would like to use it and how to make it more comfortable and warm. Think about the design elements you want to include.

Take an inventory of your essentials. Forget where everything is placed for the moment. Take a look around to determine your assets: for example, windows, or exposed brick. How do you show these off? Consider window treatments, shelving, artwork, and floor planters. Determine the practical: when the light comes into the room and from which direction, doorways, and power outlets. Then ask yourself, "Where can my furniture go that takes advantage of light and electricity, that doesn't block walkways, and where sun will not cause glare on the television or fade a wooden table?"

Think about how you hope to use the space. Do you want a cozy nook, or a space where the whole family gathers for game and movie nights? Think about the overall feel of the room—should it be calm, fun, serious, playful? Think about what makes a room more comfortable—footstools, floor pillows, side tables. Where can you put things down or stash things you use daily, like remote controls, reading glasses, and drinks?

After the practical parts, choose your favorite pieces. This can be artwork or a smaller piece of furniture or a rug—anything you're excited to showcase. It's okay if you need to see things in their place before you commit. Move things around, prop things up, get an idea for how it feels. Decide what is missing—light, weight, height, a sense of separation—and fill that void. Utilize lighting for depth and warmth. Add a tall plant to bring your eye across the room. Add a pop of color to two more dominant colors. If you have mostly wood and neutral tones, add a splash of bright color from a textile or a painting for contrast. The rule of three applies to all things in design, from photography to fashion to styling. Three objects form a pattern in our brains that forces us to see perspective. It creates interest and engagement. When in doubt, place three objects of different heights together on a surface. Hang three prints side by side.

How to hang art

Rules are meant to be broken, but they can be great guidelines. Spatial reasoning doesn't come naturally to everyone, and sometimes we can't tell why something feels just a bit off. Often, it's because we don't know or remember the rules. Artwork is measured in a gallery at eye level based on average height, but in our homes we just want it to look good over our sofas.

Try to give artwork at least 10 inches (25 cm) of space above furniture (it can be slightly more for horizontal work, slightly less for vertical). Of course, this depends on the height of your ceilings as well, and you want to make room for negative space. If your artwork is too large, your room can feel crowded or top-heavy. Also, if you

STYLE

hang your artwork too high, it can feel like it's floating. Balance is key. Artwork shouldn't be longer than the item it hangs above. Even a gallery wall should feel centered and not all-encompassing. If you decide to create a gallery wall—a grouping of a few artworks—try to leave 2 to 5 inches (5 to 12 cm) between each piece. It's often about feeling, but you must give your art room to breathe.

Space out darker pieces from one another. Mix mediums like paintings, photography, framed textiles, and shadow boxes of artifacts. If you're the kind of person who likes to *prutsen*, layer smaller pieces of art in front of larger pieces by leaning them against one another on the floor or on a shelf. It's a great way to add depth but also leave room for change. Make layered artwork look intentional by not having one piece sizably smaller than the other. Use shelves if you like the flexibility.

Table height

One of the more important rules is table height. Mostly we think it's important to have tables that are convenient. After all, that is their purpose. A good rule of thumb for side tables is that they should be equal to or slightly lower than sofa-arm height. Remember that this is a place where you will want a table lamp, maybe a stack of books, or a place to put down a drink. You want it to be accessible.

As for a coffee table, give yourself space to reach for a magazine, but enough leg room to sit comfortably. The rule here is anywhere from 14 to 18 inches (35 to 45 cm) away from seating. While the size and height can vary greatly, it's ideal if the table is slightly more than half the size of your sofa. Again, balance is key. Between furniture, you'll want 30 to 36 inches (75 to 90 cm) for pass-through space.

What to do with rugs

Our favorite rule—and favorite rule to break—is what to do with rugs. Rugs shouldn't be less than 24 inches (60 cm) away from a wall, they should rest under every piece of furniture (however slightly) and they should complement if not accentuate the room. We believe these rules are good to follow, but we also believe in layering rugs, choosing statement rugs (which are often vintage and sometimes means we want it in our house no matter what the size and fit), and even using throw blankets as floor rugs (just add a nonslip fabric underneath or use double-sided carpet tape). We have also been known to layer rugs over plain (sometimes ugly) rental-home carpets and put rugs in the kitchen to add warmth. It's okay to continuously add and subtract.

What you put into styling your space determines what you will get out of it. Be open to impulse. Delve into the details. And most importantly, trust that if you place things with intention, it will feel as such.

Now let's start styling your place. Room by room.

2
Rooms

Entrance

Chances are that your routine involves walking in and out of your front door multiple times a day—to walk the dog, drop the kids off at school, go for a run, go to work, and back again. Even if you don't have a formal entrance, this is one of the most trafficked areas in your home and it should be given some attention.

The entrance is often an indicator of how the rest of the home will feel. Personality and warmth should greet you as soon as you step through the door. Interesting objects invite you in. Intentional design makes you want to stay. This is the foundation of a well-styled home.

Stand in your entrance. Go in and out of your front door. See what it is that you're missing, what you like to put down or pick up or have handy. Is there something that makes you smile as you walk in or out? Something that makes you feel safe or loved? A gentle reminder of what home means to you? Add it. This is the space you should treat like your smartphone wallpaper. You're going to look at it constantly, so it should evoke the emotion you're seeking.

Every entrance needs a landing spot that can serve as a catchall: a surface for dropping keys, sunglasses, loose change, and mail. So there should be a tray or bowl on a table or shelf. There should be a hook to hang a bag, coat, or dog leash and a seat to put on or take off shoes. A mirror is a great addition. We like adding a small magnetized chalkboard here to share notes and humor—even if it's just hung on the back of the main door. Then you can add personal treasures to fill it out: a jar by the front door that collects bits and pieces found on wild walks or a large temple bell that rings when the door swings open.

Most entrances are tiny. And if you're working with a very small space, take advantage of the space you do have.

Use your wall space. Hang a shelf, hang some pegs, hang a mirror, hang some hooks. Nothing has to stick out very much for the few things you want to keep by the door. It can look effortlessly styled and still be functional.

If you do have room, we recommend a bench or stool as creative storage for shoes so there isn't a pile to trip over (storage baskets are great), a coco coir doormat, a coat stand and umbrella holder, and some splashes of color and personality. A lively and thoughtful entryway dotted with character is a wonderful way to step in and out of your home and will be a reminder for how to go about your day.

The entrance generally leads us into the most lived-in room.

Living Room

The living room is meant to be lived in. It should have an easy way about it with lots of options for enjoying it. If you have one room in the house you would let anyone's kids (and adults) play in, it should be this one. Don't make it too precious. Consider how you want to use the room and who will use it. Have something for everyone. This is often the room to showcase any favorites: your best art, statement pieces of furniture, collections, photographs. You'll inevitably spend a lot of time in this room, so let's make it more comfortable.

Start with your furniture. Consider the proportions of the room and the size of your furniture. If it's on the small side, try to fill it with smaller pieces—consider armless furniture and straight lines. Both of these things, along with a mirror, can make a room feel bigger. If it's a larger room, you can accommodate larger pieces. Area rugs that

are too small can make a room feel smaller. Use rugs to delineate areas. Large rugs can ground a room; long skinny rugs can lead you to the next room. Create a focal point around something like a fireplace or coffee table or your favorite piece of art.

There should always be ample seating. Have lots of different places to sit, and make sure there are options to face one another instead of just sitting side by side. And make seating close enough to each other so no one has to shout. Keep in mind everyone likes different seating arrangements, and occupants will be different ages. We are suckers for a uniquely colored vintage chair at just the right height. We also love good and thoughtful floor seating.

This room should be multipurpose. Consider ottomans, floor cushions, and side tables that double as seating or table surfaces. Be creative with what can be used as seating. The more adaptable your furniture, the more adaptable your space.

Throw cushions and blankets can make a room feel instantly inviting. They are great objects to buy on a whim and our favorite things to find while traveling. They are best in different weights, materials, sizes, and shapes. Layering textures and textiles will instantly make a room feel warmer. We often have sheepskins that move from place to place, depending on the season. Remember to mix and match; it makes your home more inviting. A good rule is to have it feel about three-quarters matching, one-quarter mixing. Like a good mixed drink, a little of the most potent goes a long way.

Now consider lighting, one of the most important elements in completing a comfortable space. Ask the same questions. What is this room for? You can use lighting to subtly differentiate parts of a room for different purposes.

Don't get stuck on what is already installed. Consider hanging pendants and using floor lamps to add height and interest to a space that feels void or dark. Table lamps are versatile and warm. Accent lights like a salt lamp or a Moroccan pendant can add interest with shadows and color. Even choosing alternative light bulbs like Edison bulbs adds impact. Using the mix-and-match approach here will offer lots of choices for creating different moods. We try to place at least two different light sources in the room: one more practical for reading by a cozy chair, and another that gives off ambient light, interesting shadows, or simply a soft glow.

Let your eyes move through the room as if it were a landscape. Create some high and low points; pair natural shapes next to the linear lines your room will inevitably have. Choose a wall to display smaller pieces of art to create a gallery wall and then hang a large piece on an adjacent wall for balance. This can potentially distract from the television as well. Mix and match frames. Reconsider what you think of as art. Frame feathers or textiles or notecards. Hang bowls, baskets, or tapestries on a wall. Layer textures and textiles.

The living room is for convening but also for stimulation. Often it houses those items you regularly turn to for inspiration—books, music, and art. Make them accessible. Cool Club playing cards or TableTopics are fun to have on the coffee table for impromptu gatherings. Always have a playlist ready for different moods. Music plays a large role in our homes. Think of the living room as an adaptable space, one that can accommodate any mood and can fit whatever needs may arise.

Lastly, we have to keep in mind life's realities—and messes. We often have food and drink in hand. Make sure your living room is prepared to handle spills and crumbs. Make space to put down a drink wherever there is seating.

How to style a coffee table

Choose four to eight objects you might like to have on the table. This can be a mixture of practical things as well as decorative objects. Try arranging them in different ways to get an idea for what will be most beautiful as well as functional.

First, try arranging them in neat quadrants or a triangular shape and then move them around to see what feels the most sensible. Step back and evaluate what it may need. Some simple additions could be a small potted plant, a tall vase, or an object of geometric or organic shape.

If the arrangement looks too cluttered, try adding a tray to catch some of the smaller things that don't add enough weight on their own. Try stacking objects. A catchall bowl or vase on top of a stack of books can consolidate space and add height and interest. And don't overlook the space you aren't using under the table. It is a perfect place to add floor cushions, short stools, or even a basket for magazines.

Your coffee table should be functional, but it is a centerpiece, and as a focal point, you should style it with consideration. ●

Try to use washable blankets and cushion covers. Technology comes with cords; hide them as best you can behind plants or tucked behind a table. Store remotes in a basket under the sofa. Plan your living space to fit real-life situations.

Which takes us neatly into the most active, accident-prone room in the house.

Kitchen

"The heart of the home," the kitchen is the gathering point for most of us. Yet it is often overlooked when it comes to styling. It can be seen as a simple and utilitarian space, but you must remember tools and utensils can be beautiful. Show off your favorite kitchenware and accessories. Everything from water filters to coffeemakers have stylish options. Look again at things you already use and own; you may have been underestimating their charm.

Chances are you have at least one wooden cutting board. Have it on display and create a vignette with a bottle of olive oil, a pinch bowl of sea salt, and a potted rosemary or thyme (hearty, useful herbs). Keep it functional and beautiful.

If you have wooden utensils, show them off and add height to your kitchen by putting them in a large utensil holder. Fill a large bowl with fruit to add color and texture. This room should be treated with the same attentiveness as any other room in the house. Add artwork to the walls, hang a plant, place a stool that doubles as a chair in the corner. Hang handmade tea towels.

If you like the look of your glasses or dishes, set them out on an open shelf. Place objects next to your favorite cookbooks. Styling your kitchen shelves should be treated the same as styling your living room shelves.

Jars can look beautiful on open shelves. They're also a great ally in the kitchen. You can bottle, store leftovers, pour drinks, or use them as makeshift vases. You can store bulk grains, salts, or flours. Stack smaller jars on open shelving for attractive and smart storage. They can be old spaghetti-sauce jars or Mason jars. They're eye-catching and we cook more simply because they act as a visual reminder of what ingredients we have. They look great lined up in a row, labeled (or not) and ready for use.

Biodegradable sponges and brushes with wooden handles are so much more attractive (and better for the environment). We put ours in vintage dishes and vases by the sink. Dish soap can be poured into decorative soap dispensers. This also gives you the opportunity to buy in bulk to save money and use less plastic. This is our recipe for a creative and considered life: Find sustainable solutions for your home and life, use them creatively, and style them thoughtfully.

The kitchen is one of the most forgiving rooms, because it does need to be so functional. So mix it up a bit. Style your breakfast bar or kitchen table with mismatched linen napkins, unique salt and pepper shakers, a vase with fresh-cut flowers, and some candles in vintage or modern candleholders.

Try to keep it clean. The tidier you keep it, the more likely you'll be able to enjoy it. We always try to leave our sinks dish-free. The less daunting the kitchen feels at the end of the day (and at the beginning), the more likely we'll be inspired to cook in it.

If your kitchen doesn't have a table to sit at or you're in need of a larger space, we can spill into the next room . . .

Dining Room

Generally, this is the room that contains the large dining room table, chairs, and maybe a bar cart or drinks trolley. This is a room for sharing. This is where we break bread, toast special occasions, and celebrate.

If you have a square or rectangular table, try to add rounded elements to soften things up. In any room, you do not want all straight lines. This is a perfect room to keep furniture simple but highlight great wall pieces. It should feel like you can host a celebratory dinner or a spontaneous and informal get-together. Mix all levels of décor—high-end and low-end objects like fancy china with thrift store glasses. Make it feel special and uniquely yours.

Also mix and match chairs when possible. Consider putting a bench at one end. Add accent and comfort pieces like sheepskin or cushions. We'll go into how to style a table more in the hosting section, but try to keep a simple centerpiece and candles on the table. Indoor/outdoor rugs are great in dining rooms where spills are most common. Rugs should sit at least 24 inches (60 cm) wider than your table but still be at least 8 inches (10 cm) from the walls.

Most importantly, make sure the lighting is ample enough to see the food and one another, but isn't blinding, as some overhead lighting can be. Lighting is worth investing in here. Lights should hang 30 to 36 inches (75 to 90 cm) above the table. If you are renting, use pendants with cloth-wrapped cord to help them blend in. If you own your home, install a dimmer and get yourself a statement piece, like a chandelier, that becomes the centerpiece of the room. It's worth the investment if you eat here at all. Lighting changes the entire mood of a dinner party—even if it's just a party for two.

A makeshift bar can be a beautiful addition with glasses and different drinks. This could be on top of a sideboard or on a drinks trolley or bar cart. Elevate it by transferring spirits to decanters and hang metal labels around their necks. This is where we prefer our largest and boldest artwork and the most delicate items on shelves, since it's rare that the dining room turns into a playroom.

Now, let's get to work.

Home Office

Many of us work from home these days, either one or two days a week or full time. Often we don't have the luxury of having a dedicated room for this. The reality is that our home office often doubles as a guest room, play area, or storage space. Regardless, it still needs to encourage productivity. The goal is to find the balance where the room can have multiple uses if necessary, but still allow us to get work done.

Key to this is organization. First, find a space with natural light, calm colors, and—most importantly—quiet. If the room is multipurpose, then create a work space near to the window and close to a power outlet to charge all your gadgets. Give yourself plenty of storage options for paperwork: baskets, boxes, crates, shelves. You'll be sitting down for potentially long periods, so your priority is a desk for your computer (you can make your own by getting the exact size of wood you need cut and adding it to hairpin or sawhorse legs) and a chair that is comfortable, sturdy, and the right height for your desk.

Then think about the spaces around the desk. Can you spread out if you need to? Perhaps there is an option for a pullout from the desk to create an additional work surface. Or a chest of drawers with a large surface area on top to spread out paperwork. Use your wall space, too. Hang a calendar, add a bookshelf, have a wall that doubles as a mood board—and whatever else may entice you to look up every couple of hours from the computer screen to inspire rather than distract you.

Be mindful that this room more than any is where we administrate our lives, so it is prone to clutter. And as it just keeps coming, you need to have a system that allows you to quickly and easily deal with it or dispose of it.

Clutter is not only distracting on our desk but also in our minds. A Princeton University Neuroscience Institute study found people with cluttered homes experience greater exhaustion and stress. The chaos restricts your ability to focus and limits your brain's ability to process information. The awareness of clutter wears down your mental state, which leads to frustration and poor decision-making.

We all do it. Piles of receipts, books we haven't read, things we've collected but just can't get rid of because of some attachment we can't shake. As the digital world continues to expand, we are now not only fighting the clutter of physical objects, but digital ones as well. Notifications, emails, text messages . . . the more our brain has to filter, the less effective it is.

Clutter—and our threshold for it—means something different for everyone, but do yourself a favor and keep your office (and life) as clutter-free as reasonably possible.

Try these simple solutions to keep things from piling up:

1. Organize your emails and computer desktop daily
Set aside a specific time to check email. Unless you have a job that requires you to be on call at every moment, you'll

be far more productive and focused if you fix a set amount of time (e.g., first thing in the morning, after lunch, before the end of the day) to sort, organize, and respond to emails. In almost all mailboxes, there are options to color-code or prioritize or filter email into folders. Take the time to unsubscribe from junk mail, move emails into a folder that will need eventual responses, and respond to urgent requests. Set an automatic response if you would prefer to check (and be expected to respond) only once a day.

Just like your email, at the end of your workday, it is a great idea to sort through your computer and make sure you delete unnecessary files, move everything into specific folders, and complete a backup of the work you did that day.

2. Create a daily and weekly timeline

Setting a loose (or tight) schedule is a great way to increase productivity. What are your tasks for the day? Do you have important deadlines to hit? It's important to keep an updated calendar. Choose a planner or calendar that works for you (digital or paper). Do you need something portable, where you can jot down ideas and reminders? If it's digital, do you want notifications and for it to merge lists, tasks, and appointments? Do you want a wall or desk calendar you can constantly look at? Whatever you do, be fair to yourself and make sure your timeline targets are realistic.

3. Use small storage spaces

Consuming less is always helpful. Try to take the time to put things away into their respective places. Have a receipt box, a paperwork box, an office supplies box. Be creative here by using well-designed boxes or wooden drawers as storage. Decide what you need to have on hand and find clever places to keep everything organized (paper clips, color-coded folders, wire baskets, file boxes).

4. Leave things tidy

A few minutes spent tidying at the end of the day will pay dividends. If you take the time to clean up before you leave, it will be a more welcoming and productive space to walk into the next day. This goes hand in hand with the previous three solutions. The key is to be mindful of a mess (this applies to all aspects of life).

Do Breathe: Calm your mind. Find focus. Get stuff done. by Michael Townsend Williams offers great insight on how to cultivate good habits and improve workflow and focus.

Now let's go somewhere quiet and unplug.

Bedroom

We begin and end our day in the bedroom. We spend about a third of our lives there. So this room requires some attention. You must find a balance between creating a sanctuary for effortless mornings and soothing evenings. Colors should be somewhat muted, artwork should not be too bold. It's best if you can keep technology—especially televisions—outside your bedroom. Rely on feng shui basics. Determine an element (fire, earth, metal, water, wood) and let that guide the color scheme and energy of the room.

To create a serene space, lighting again is a key factor. Your bedroom should have a light you can read by, preferably one where you can have the bulb not facing you that can also dim or at least turn on and off easily. If possible, angle overhead lighting away from the bed. If you are tight for space on your nightstand, hang or use wall-mounted lighting as an alternative.

Make space for morning meditation (even if that's just a deep breath and a morning stretch), and place a dressing gown or sweater by your bedside so your excuse for staying under the covers is lessened. Make your bed as soon as you get up—when our rooms are tidy, our day can start off less hectic and with more intention. *New York Times* bestselling author of *The Happiness Project*, Gretchen Rubin, says that making your bed is one of the simplest habits you can adopt to effectively boost happiness. By accomplishing this task first thing in the morning, you set the tone for the entire day. A National Sleep Foundation poll also found survey participants who reportedly made their beds were more likely to say they got a good night's sleep. Small actions, like details, can make a big difference.

Just as you design your bedroom for mornings, you will need to design it for evenings. It's a fine balance. There is a tone to set for the ritual of sleep. Take care to have all the things that make a bedroom comfortable within arm's reach. Keep slippers next to your bed, tissues nearby in a wooden box, and a carafe of water on your bedside table (this can be something as simple as an old gin bottle), along with a good pile of books and maybe even a journal (try *Keel's Simple Diary* and *One Line a Day: A Five-Year Memory Book*). Keep essential oil in a vintage glass bottle (apply bergamot to the bottom of your feet before bed for a better night's sleep). Headboards can be a great centerpiece styled for sleep and design. Consider alternatives to traditional headboards, like framed art, floating shelves, or even an old (properly treated) barn door. Make it a space that grounds you.

Linen and bedding are obviously an essential part of the bedroom, but it pays to experiment with different types of pillows (buckwheat is hypoallergenic and often grown organically). Choose sheets made from a material like linen that will keep you cool in the summer and warm in the winter. Bedding is one of our greatest indulgences. Finding a great duvet with just the right amount of fluff and then trying different covers can be a dramatic and affordable way to change the whole feel of a room. Don't underestimate the impact of throw cushions and adding a blanket at the end of the bed. Choose an unexpected color or pattern; make sure it's comfortable and comforting.

For all the days that can't begin and end so tidily, it is essential to create a way to accommodate life. For instance, a leaning ladder or an over-the-door hook where you can drape your clothes instead of hanging them up right away. An attractive box with a lid for unsightly things like earplugs, hand lotion, or an eye mask. Or a tray to catch the remains of your pockets.

The bedroom is a room where you want to induce serenity. This is a room where you can use darker colors to make it feel more intimate. Take advantage of different textures and warmer textiles. Keep artwork to a minimum to reduce stimulation. Let this be a room for peace and rejuvenation. Greenery in the bedroom can purify the air and make the room feel fresh: spider plant, dracaena, ficus, snake plant, peace lily, aloe vera, and bamboo palm are among the best air purifiers. This should be the calmest room in your home.

Outside the personal quiet space of the bedroom, let's move on to an often shared and less talked-about room.

Bathroom

The bathroom can actually be an extension of the bedroom. It is a room where you welcome privacy, quietude, and, of course, functionality. Regardless of windows, you should attempt to create a bathroom that is bright, lively, and luxurious.

Enhance your bathroom. Light fixtures, hardware, and paint color may seem daunting to change, but can elevate your space (even a rental) from one you tolerate to one you love. The simple act of stacking pretty towels and hanging eucalyptus from the shower are great, easy ways to make the bathroom feel like the spa. Find an attractive soap dispenser; add scented candles. When in doubt, add greenery. Air plants love the bathroom for the moisture, as do aloe, ferns, and pothos. Not only do they add life but also freshness.

Treat this room like you would any other, but remember to plan a space for putting clothes down or hanging an extra towel. Have practical storage solutions for extra toilet paper (in the cabinet, in a basket), extra towels (stacked on a floating shelf, hung over the tub), and toothbrushes and toothpaste (in a porcelain or cement cup). Is there room for a ladder to hang your clothes? A basket to put laundry?

This is a room you must continuously use to feel what's perfect and what's missing. Much like the entrance, you will be in and out of here often. Take notice of what it needs and style it accordingly based on function and beauty. This is also a room where many of us appreciate some humor in the form of a funny book or framed cartoon.

Now on to our favorite space.

Outdoors

We don't all have large and lovely back gardens; some of us have only patios or porches. Regardless of size, the outdoors always makes us feel whole. Try to take advantage of any outdoor space you have and make it a true extension of your home.

Our goal is always to create a living room, outside. From potted plants, to an herb garden, to waterproof chairs, we use our outdoor space as a retreat to reflect, have a glass of wine, start our morning, end our day, read a book, take a nap.

With that in mind, try to find space for a hammock, meditation stools, or a small table to put coffee on. Think about where to find sun or shade. If you can find a way, an outdoor shower or tub are true luxuries. An outdoor space is simply another room to escape to. Apply all the same rules for styling your living area but with many more plants. Take notice of the change of seasons. Grow moss underfoot during the autumn and winter. Set the table for spring and summer meals. Hang wind chimes and bistro lights. Use solar lights that automatically turn on once the sun sets to invite outdoor dining when the weather permits. And to ensure you make the most out of a gathering, find a space for a firepit with plenty of mobile seating (tree stumps, lounge chairs, wicker stools) and stack a pile of outdoor throw blankets.

Perspective, as always, is what you need when styling. Make sure you're constantly stepping back and seeing where your eye falls. Use the space you're styling and take note of what's missing, what would be helpful, what's too much. This is true when bringing the outside in, and equally so when bringing the indoors out.

And remember, nature never goes out of style.

3
Nature

Study nature, love nature,
stay close to nature.
It will never fail you.

Frank Lloyd Wright

Bringing the outside in is at the core of our design style. Not simply because it's beautiful, or can introduce great texture and tones, but because it keeps us grounded and connected to the Earth. Surrounding ourselves and designing with beauty from the outdoors makes us happier, healthier, and calmer. Noticing the colors, structure, and growth of flora and incorporating that into our spaces can cultivate more than just creativity. It can cultivate style.

It may not be for everyone, but our style stems from nature. We love finding feathers, stones, and shells. We can't stop putting seedpods in vessels and branches on shelves, or hanging sticks from ceilings and walls. We make lighting from fallen birch trees and tree roots. Tree stumps serve as our end tables and double as perfect solutions for outdoor seating. We style every space with the love of nature in mind. It is truly a wild habit. We work to incorporate nature into a space, but not overwhelm it. We are continually inspired by being outside and finding ways to design products and spaces that reflect that.

Forest Bathing

Shinrin-yoku is a Japanese term that means "taking in the forest atmosphere" or "forest bathing." Developed in the 1980s, it has become a cornerstone of preventive health care and healing in Japanese medicine. The aim of forest bathing is to slow down and become immersed in the natural environment. Your task at hand is to use all your senses. A study published by the National Center for Biotechnology Information compared a city walk to a forest walk. The amount of activity was equal, but researchers found the forest environment led to significant reductions in blood pressure and certain stress hormones. It only takes fifteen minutes of walking outdoors to produce results.

Forest bathing's official site says a walk in the forest will boost your immune system and improve mood, sleep, and energy levels. "Go to a forest. Walk slowly. Breathe. Open all your senses. This is the healing way of Shinrin-yoku Forest Therapy, the medicine of simply being in the forest."

If you take the lessons learned from forest bathing and do nothing more than pay attention, you'll achieve a more creative and considered life. Nature is boundless. There are hundreds and thousands of cues to take from the Earth. If you look closely, you'll see a very delicate balance of how and where things grow, and patterns in all living things. There is no shortage of inspiration. The more in touch you are with nature, the more in tune you are with life.

Styling Advice

Have an open mind about what is beautiful. You don't have to be in the most exotic wild places to find highly compelling objects. Take a walk along a path you frequently use and really pay attention. You will find inspiration in colors, shapes, and patterns. Look up and down, notice what colors you like, what shapes you like, whether you prefer the feeling of being sheltered by trees or the freedom of vast open fields. Do you prefer bright and sunny days, or when the weather turns moody and gray? Once you identify what you like, you can re-create these moods in different parts of your home with the use of color, texture, space, and light.

One of the easiest styling rules to follow is to style from floor to ceiling, dark to light. We call this Nature's Rule of Light. Keep the floor the darkest (the Earth itself), then as our eye travels upward toward the ceiling, have it get slightly brighter (through the trees) and lighter (toward the sky). Some rules are meant to be broken, but we love the basis of this one.

Natural light

Allow natural light to guide a room. If you prefer being sheltered, consider creating a quiet space to work or read in a room you can paint a dark blue or green, where natural light from a window is minimal. If light is brightest where you want it to be darkest, consider dark wood blinds. But for all other spaces, use natural window light to your advantage. It always accentuates the beauty of a room—even those painted in dark hues. Install muslin curtains for privacy while allowing the most light to enter.

When natural light is hard to come by, add artificial light to change the ambience. Light fixtures that point upward can compensate for little light in the room, as can shiny surfaces like translucent tables and metallic shelves. Hang mirrors opposite windows and, if you really like a warm room, consider off-white paint colors with a satin finish. By adding color and contrast, a room will naturally feel warmer. Take advantage of shadows and reflections created by your décor or objects placed by windows, or even from the trees outside. Let natural light add a playful and artful element to your space.

Natural resources

By looking for inspiration whenever you step outside, you can add a sense of wonder to your life and a piece of nature to your home. Be amazed by the shapes and colors of nature. This is where spontaneity comes in. Look for things that interest you. A foraged branch is our go-to object. When placed inside, it has an immediate impact with its unique shape and the unpredictable way it takes up space. An old piece of driftwood can be a table centerpiece. You can hang lights from a large sun-bleached branch or stand it upright in a corner. You can hang any branch on a wall or use it as a display for jewelry.

We often pick up stones on our travels—from beaches, lakes, the woods. From Iceland, we bought stones made from fabric, delicately crocheted by a local artist. They sit on our desks as a reminder that Earth's natural resources will always be the most beautiful, but they can also be enhanced. Use this natural beauty in your home. Place striped stones in a bowl, in a sink, next to the bathtub, or use them as a door-stopper. Place wild findings on a shelf, or on a stack of books, or hang them on a wall.

There are no boundaries between you and nature. It's easy to make beauty from that which is already so beautiful.

Materials

When thinking of bigger pieces that can't be picked up casually on a walk, there are plenty of natural materials you can bring into your home to make it feel more organic.

Wood is the perfect material. It is warm and easy, with a wide variety of species and applications. It can be raw or finished, found or bought, and is always durable and appealing. Reclaimed wood is a great solution for "rustic meets modern." It's sustainable and has incredible character. It is hard to deny the beauty in the grain and in the story of where it came from. We can see and feel this overwhelming sense of beauty in history and design when we visit places like Hill of the Hawk House in Big Sur, built from the wood of a bridge that crossed the Russian River in California and standing as majestically today as it did when it was first built in 1966.

Copper is a great complement to wood. It's modern but rustic with the power to add a little shine without being overly showy. The patina of an old copper pot can be the perfect place for a houseplant, or an easily obtained copper pipe can hold hanging kitchen tools or towels. It can also be a good alternative for surfaces if you already have a lot of wood pieces. We both have copper dining tables that only get more beautiful over time.

Greenery

If you ever feel something is lacking, add a plant. It is the most affordable and beautiful way to add texture, shape, and color to any space. Houseplants breathe life into a home. Literally. Our go-to easy-to-care-for houseplants include philodendron, dracaena, echeveria, aloe, ficus, cacti, and our new favorite, marimo balls.

Plants can be used as room dividers. Very large plants are a work of art in themselves, and a real statement piece, a living sculpture. Plants are organic mobiles and great for spaces small and large. They can be mounted to a wall, clustered on shelves, and treated as indoor gardens.

Pots don't necessarily have to be used as plant holders. Think outside the box. Consider plants in bowls or vases, aquatic plants, grouping multiple plants together, terrariums, and mixing and matching colors and textures and materials. The green will tie them together.

The more we connect with nature, the more we will feel the urgency to care for it. As you gain inspiration from the beauty of the Earth, be mindful of what you are taking and what you are willing to give back. Always forage responsibly, and when you bring home your treasures and perhaps put a felled lichen-covered stick on the shelf, remember that it was a life and now is living with you. Nature is quite generous with us. Let's try to show the same courtesy.

How to go on a wild walk

On any walk, we love picking up stones, branches, moss, and seedpods. For us, foraging is second nature. If it doesn't come as naturally to you, the first step is to go outside. Often. Take a walk with no expectations. Wander freely. If you are on a specific foraging mission, you can take a tote, some clippers, and a pair of gardening gloves. Pay attention. Look at whatever interests you. Remember to look in all directions. Cut some greenery, pick up sticks, keep an eye out for feathers on the ground. Look for things that have naturally fallen or may have dried with the change of seasons. There is always opportunity to see the beauty in nature and find a place for it in your home. As your collection grows, you can move or replace the items.

All of these natural treasures can be placed in trays or vases or perched on top of frames. We like to stack a few stones the same way we stack books. Keep a vase on hand that holds your dried pods. Pair them with things you've dried yourself that hold up, such as *Craspedia*—the bright yellow Billy Buttons—lavender, and eucalyptus.

Each walk you take can be a wild one filled with hidden treasures if you pay attention to everything around you. ●

4
Senses

I go to nature to be soothed and healed,
and have my senses put in order.

John Burroughs

Design is inherently better when it induces feeling.
When styling your space, think about utilizing *all* of
your senses to make it feel complete. By doing this,
you will enhance the overall "experience" of your space
and, in turn, how you and your family or passing
guests feel when they spend time there. By activating
all five senses—sight, sound, smell, touch, and taste—
you can really alter or create a mood.

To get started, consider an experience or memory you
really cherish. Ask yourself how this might have
shaped you, your values, and your aesthetics. Replay the
experience in your mind using these prompts:

I saw . . .

I heard . . .

I smelled . . .

I touched . . .

I tasted . . .

Here are a couple of our own to help you get started:

DQ: I remember the first time I went to my cousin Jane's apartment in New York City. I was probably around twelve years old, very impressionable and very unstylish. It was winter and we trudged up the eight floors and found ourselves walking into a sensory wonderland. She welcomed us with hot cocoa served in vintage teacups. She took our coats and hung them in her bedroom closet among vintage silk nightgowns. It was the most fanciful wardrobe I'd ever seen. I sat in wonder looking around at all the books piled up high, small treasures nestled among them: antique figurines, handwritten postcards, dried flowers on the shelves. The scent of candles and fresh flowers was perfectly subtle.

I sat on an oversized pillow on the floor, next to the mother-of-pearl tiled bathtub (which was in the kitchen), and listened as she told us stories about the place when it was completely run-down, zoning in and out with the Brazilian jazz she had playing in the background. She made us feel warm and special—as if we had been let into a secret place filled with very personal treasures. She has that way about her, red lipstick and all, and that is how I knew what style was—and that she had it. Her home existed exactly the way that she did—full of intricacies, extraordinary, and very entertaining. I've been back to visit many times since and the allure has not worn off. Each time I find something new, clever, and beautiful.

SF: I come from a tidy family, mostly because we're all from Hong Kong, where space and solitude are a complete luxury. When you live in two hundred square feet, there isn't room to make a mess. My family always lived incredibly intentionally. My parents are both handy (mostly out of necessity) and taught me the importance of details. They took time to show me the beauty in calligraphy, artwork, woodwork, music, history, my elders, adventure, and karma. I left Hong Kong a long time ago, but I can still feel the heat and humidity, can still smell my aunt's cooking.

I go back often. I find peace in the commotion, I feel invigorated by the lights and energy, I can taste street food just walking by, and I can smell the Dettol every family uses to clean the floors each evening after dinner when the tables are put away to make room for living space.

Today, I see how these experiences shaped me and how I balance my aesthetics with my pining for both the city and the wild. In the Pacific Northwest, where I live now, I hear the coyotes in the night. I fully experience and can sense the seasons change. I eat from the life that grows around me. This was in me all along. It comes from my father's side: the farmers and wanderers. My style stems from this dichotomy. Old with new, East with West, city with rural. I crave the sensory overload. I need all my senses filled in my life as I do in my home.

When we tune in to all our senses—rather than just our visual sense—we start to engage in the space around us. We become more present, creative, and stimulated. Much like forest bathing, we experience our immediate space with a new perspective.

Whether you are adding herbs under your showerhead, painting an accent wall, draping voile from a bed canopy, displaying sentimental photographs, or filling your basin with stones, every detail you add encourages you and those you share your home with to pay attention. Each room should evoke all five senses.

Sight

Sight is such an important sense when it comes to style. By playing with color, you can create subtle triggers with this sense in order to cultivate a mood where you can do the things you want to do and feel the way you'd like to feel.

Color has an almost immediate impact. It has an obvious way of making a statement, affecting or reflecting our mood, and can set the stage for your spaces. The color of your space will be the foundation on which to add details, show off your statement pieces, and set the tone for the overall feeling of your home.

Are you drawn to the soft color of a eucalyptus leaf or the bright splash of a hibiscus? You can introduce pops of color as accent and attitude, or induce calm with more neutral tones. Bright colors excite, while warm colors relax. Consider your home office or studio. Green sparks creativity. White reduces distraction, but teal inspires. These colors don't have to overwhelm. They can be as simple and small as the color of your mood board rather than an entire room. Gray and blue are calming colors. Perhaps it's worth investing in bedding in these hues.

When we decide on styling with color, we try to stick to the rule of 60–30–10. Keep 60 percent of the space a dominant color (off-white or dark navy walls), 30 percent in secondary colors (a gray sofa or walnut furniture), and 10 percent accent colors (a handwoven Hmong textile pillow cover, a brass vase, brightly colored coffee table books).

Sound

If you've ever been moved by the perfect song or gone mad because of noisy pipes, you know the power sound can have over your spirit and well-being. This sense can transport you.

According to *Two Awesome Hours: Science-Based Strategies to Harness Your Best Time and Get Your Most Important Work Done* by Josh Davis, environmental noise—background music, city sounds, people's conversations—reduces productivity for most people. And while some background noise can improve positivity and increase performance, it often disrupts more thoughtful tasks like reading. Quiet spaces win.

Next time you are home alone, really listen. Recognize the parts that are charming (the sounds of an old clock) and the ones that aren't (a squeaky door and creaky floorboards). Distractions are often unavoidable, but there are some tricks to make them less intrusive.

Create quiet spaces away from windows that face a street, boilers, or refrigerator hums. Soft materials, rugs, textiles, and upholstered furniture all absorb sound. If you have any windows on a busy street, consider thick window treatments like wool. Invest some time in greasing your door hinges. If you have squeaky old floors, rub baby powder or baking soda into the seams to keep the boards from rubbing together.

Much more adaptable than taking away noise, adding noise can be your solution to help you focus, enjoy your space, write, dance, or socialize. Playing classical and ambient music is how we wrote this book! Try to use music, white noise from an app, or natural elements to drown out the noise distracting you. Or just to set the mood. We've put together some playlists that you'll find in the Resources section at the back of the book.

Touch

Touch can invoke a simple and immediate response. It affects how we respond to a room and can determine how we spend time in it. Texture is what will warm your space, spark interest, and make a room complete. Texture can come from textiles, rugs, plants, furniture, and even the architecture of the room itself. Layer all of these to create a space you don't want to leave.

Think about a living room with a soft loveseat with wooden armrests. Consider an office with a shaggy cushion on a leather chair in front of a black wall with a wooden trolley carrying metal baskets and a decanter tray. Try a jute rug under your wood and copper kitchen table, mismatched chairs, and a bench draped in sheepskin along either side, a wild fern in a macramé plant hanger hung low from the ceiling corner. Have succulents dot the windowsill. Make each knob on your drawers unique. All of these vignettes are designed to be touched.

We constantly find ourselves drawn to wool blankets and scarves. These unique handcrafted pieces can add real character when placed in a room—draped over the arm of a sofa or placed at the end of a bed. We look for block prints to frame and kilim to make pillows out of. Natural dyed linens make great additions to the kitchen either as tablecloths or napkins. We love splashes of color to complement our metal cabinets, wooden tables, and neutral sofas.

Just as we ourselves are not defined by one style, our homes are also not defined by a single style. We encourage you to layer different textures, artifacts from different countries, different colors, different styles. Complicated textures garner curiosity and beckon to be enjoyed. It reminds us of the tapestry of life. These are the elements to a beautiful room.

Taste

While not always the first sense that comes to mind when thinking about interior design, taste is one that undoubtedly enhances an experience.

When setting up an event, hosting a dinner party, or even enjoying a casual dinner at home, it is equally important to take note both of what is being served and what the food is being served on. Flavors and themes will influence how a table should be set (see "How to Style a Table" on page 107), what lighting to use, what dishware to choose, and how décor is adorned.

Having a child's birthday party? Perhaps the fine china goes away. Colorful linens and lots of hand snacks can come out. Hosting a dinner with neighbors and friends? Offer a help-yourself drinks bar and a large cheese plate (see "How to Style a Cheeseboard" on page 107). Just want to add taste to your everyday life? Keep a bowl of fresh clementines on the table to encourage healthy snacking while also adding a pop of color.

Smell

Our sense of smell is perhaps our most evocative sense. It can transform a space by altering how we feel in it. According to an article Christopher Bergland wrote in *Psychology Today*, smell is our most primal sense. Scents have the power to drive our behavior on an instinctive and subconscious level. Smells can trigger forgotten memories and influence the appeal of a place or product. You can use fragrance as a tool to create a state of mind.

We want our kitchens to smell inviting, our offices to boost productivity, our bathrooms to be fresh, our bedrooms to be soothing. Scents have the power to influence emotion. They can help our well-being. If we smell something we find pleasant, it can have a positive effect on the mind and adjust our mood.

Adding scent is the simplest way to bring a sensory experience into your daily life. Burning candles or incense, using room diffusers, and setting out flower arrangements and herbs are all effective methods.

Place lavender sachets in bedrooms for relaxation. Many companies now make aromatherapy room sprays. You can use these or make your own with essential oils. Give yourself an energy boost in the morning by tying lemon balm or eucalyptus under your showerhead (out of the way of the water stream) and let the heat of your shower release the refreshing oils from the leaves. Add joy and color to your living room by putting fresh-cut flowers on the table (some of our favorites: lilac, peony, hyacinth, jasmine). Cut bergamot or peppermint from your garden and hang them with twine upside down to dry in your kitchen to boost energy. Burn a cedarwood or neroli candle in your living room to relieve tension. If you're feeling a bit down, use geranium or sage scents. The best scent of all? Fresh air. Remember to open your windows and air out the house every so often.

We are always trying to stimulate all our senses, whether we're styling a space, throwing a dinner party, or simply longing for something pleasant to come home to at the end of a hectic day. It's a lovely way to go about life. Remember to consider other factors, like sentiment, nostalgia, serenity, and humor, as sensibilities that you want your space to reflect. There's so much beauty in the details.

Details may be perceived as small, but they are a large part of what makes your house a home. When styled well, it is the details that make a significant statement and that make your space unique. They will define it. Details are what will spark a memory or make a difference. It's what people respond to and remember.

Details don't just begin and end with well-chosen artwork or design elements. It is everything in between. It comes from *prutsen*. It's the how and the why. When you start to look at every part of an object—and each room as an opportunity for beauty—your space will start to feel full and even necessary. It's the joy you find in the small ring dish you have by the sink given to you by your best friend, or your grandfather's wooden screwdriver in your tool drawer. It isn't just a stack of books; it's the choice of books you love and want to showcase, and the feather bookmark you use to save your place.

Such details hold sentiment and stories. These are the things that will fill your space, draw you in, and keep you still. When you style with purpose, with a *raison d'être*, you are putting more consideration into your home and into your life. Paying attention is inherently creative. You are giving your things a sense of belonging and a place to belong.

DQ: I have a stick that has traveled with me everywhere I've lived. It is a walking stick my dad carved while camping over twenty years ago. It is plain, mostly straight, and isn't of much note other than it hangs on a wall. It doesn't have any intricate detail or even make much of a statement, but it has been the centerpiece of my home for as long as I can remember. Just as his memory that lives in it is most certainly the centerpiece of my life. This is detail, the things that add not only to the atmosphere of your home but also to the sentiment of your life.

SF: I have a hand-forged feather that sits on my desk. I remember so clearly the blacksmith who made it and the moments between it being made and being handed to me. I'm transported back in time to that day. It reminds me of kindness. It's most often these small details and objects that bring me the greatest joy and elicit the sweetest memories. These are the things and the feelings I take note of when I step into someone else's space. It makes paying attention so worthwhile.

Much like a handwritten note, when you take the extra time and extra effort to style your spaces, it doesn't go unnoticed. By determining what is necessary, what pieces you enjoy and prioritizing what matters, you give your home and your objects room to shine and breathe.

Detailing Do USA

On a beautiful farm and winery in Hopland, California, along the banks of the Russian River, sits Campovida— host to the Do Lectures USA. Here, people care about the detail—especially owners Anna and Gary.

Every year, tepees are erected for the eighty attendees of the four-day event. These tents are a blank canvas. Literally. Each tent starts with a dirt floor and canvas sides with big, beautiful wood beams to hold it all together. With the help of many creative minds and helping hands, we assess what we have and what we will use to make this the most comfortable camping experience for the attendees.

We begin by applying the same principles of how to style a bedroom. We start with furniture. We have cots, hay bales, throw rugs, blankets, a great wild garden. We use the cots and put together the bedding. Soft, clean sheets, a nicely made bed layered with a wool blanket, with a lavender pouch on the pillow. We add a place to set personal items on a stump next to the bed. We place a glass jug of water, a flashlight by the tepee door, and a votive candle for ambience. A welcome note, a map, and a schedule lets you know you are welcome and taken care of.

Final steps range from the practical to the luxurious— hanging a bouquet of flowers from the center of each tepee and smudging the interiors with palo santo sticks (a cleansing holy wood found in South America that smells of pine, mint, and citrus). A hay bale covered with a blanket sits outside as a space to take off your shoes, stargaze, and reflect on the day. You can start from nothing and create something beautiful and thoughtful. Just add detail.

DETAIL

When you pay attention to what makes a space feel perfect, it's knowing there's a story behind the objects placed around the room. It's the side table at just the right height for you to leave a drink, the cozy blanket draped over a sofa to keep your toes warm, the soft pillow to lay your head on. There's stimulating artwork, calm colors, a cool breeze, warm scents. These details come from the way you have thought about how to style the room and from how you have stimulated all five senses. It connects you to place, it's lit perfectly, and there's just the right amount of greenery. It's your photography, your keepsakes. You thought of every detail.

Now you have to decide how you're going to share it.

6
Share

Living together is an art.

William Pickens

It's more common than not to have to share our homes with housemates, partners, children. You want to create a home that feels just right, but it also needs to feel right for those you live with, too. When sharing a home, we have to consider the needs of everyone around us. It's actually a great lesson in how to live. Your home can still have character, style, and cohesion. Sometimes it just takes a little compromise.

Think about and determine the needs and priorities of those you share your space with. Be considerate of each other and thoughtful of the other person's likes, wants, and needs alongside your own. Most importantly, be tidy. The more people you share your home with, the more challenging this becomes. Try. No matter who you're living with, make designated places for all the practical things. Make a shelf for linens and extra toiletries. Make it obvious where dishes, mugs, and cutlery go. Create a space for spices and snacks, for piles of books, for mail, keys, and bags. The more organized your home is, the more everyone can work at keeping it that way and the more put-together it will feel.

Living with . . .

Partners

Sharing your life means sharing your things. If you're moving in together for the first time, it's likely you'll both already have some furniture. Take an inventory of what you have, what you need, and what you can get rid of. Go through a checklist of what each person values—this can mean both aesthetically (minimalist versus maximalist, color and art preferences, what's beautiful versus what's comfortable) and financially (how much do you want to spend on new things for your new space together?).

Make sure you purge with consideration and attention to detail. Maybe one sofa is more interesting, but the other fits better. Maybe one coffee table is nicer, but the other is an heirloom. Be fair. Be empathetic. We are often very tied to our things for reasons we sometimes can't explain. Make sure you each know what matters the most to you. Vintage cordial glasses on a mid-century modern sideboard can also house a bobblehead collection. You can evolve your tastes together. Balance is a beautiful thing.

Housemates

The healthiest way to share a home is to share your priorities. Communicate. If you're moving into a home with friends or acquaintances, you may have to compromise on whose furniture to keep or what to buy. Because you likely won't live together forever, be practical and considerate. If you have a piece you love that doesn't fit into the communal areas, maybe it goes in your bedroom.

Embrace your own corners. Your bedroom will be your sanctuary, so make it feel the way you need to be comfortable. We've found some people care more about one room than another. Split the difference. Your shared home should be accessible, functional, and fun. As you mix and match your décor, know that it's adding life to a home.

Children

Between crayons, toys, blocks, and books, sharing life with children can feel overwhelming—and interior design might be the last thing on your mind. Creative storage will be your greatest asset here, and having practical solutions in communal rooms means a quick tidy doesn't take up too much of your already depleted energy. Not having to look at kids' clutter, even for a brief moment in the evening, can provide some respite and help you reclaim your space—albeit temporarily. Make sure there is a toy chest for all the stray bits and bobs. Have deep drawers to hide the mess.

And try to embrace the chaos (a little). Create a low shelf for a few items a child can reach—maybe the handmade wooden whale on wheels you played with as a child that is now one of their favorites. Piles of children's books can be as aesthetically pleasing as coffee table books.

DQ: As someone who has a strong sense of style and likes to be surrounded by my own things, sharing is a daily struggle. Currently, I'm living in a small home with a partner, a big dog, and a baby. Trying to decide what to give up and where to give in is a challenge. Yet, I do find that it has made me more decisive and more creative in my space. So while, ideally, I'd have a studio space, extra bedrooms, a bigger kitchen, and more storage, working within the boundaries of a thousand square feet keeps me

resourceful. I'm constantly finding ways to store things under furniture (wood boxes under my couch, under cabinets, stacked in closets), while still trying to keep things looking how I'd like them to look.

SF: I love my own corners. I don't mind sharing because I'm constantly creating small vignettes that are mine alone. I keep a few favorite things in a tray, on my desk or on my nightstand, in my drawers or in my bag, and that's enough for me. I've lived on boats, in tiny apartments, in a converted chicken shed on a farm, in a yurt. Style and personality always emerge. Of course, I prefer having a space that is my own (my office is usually my favorite room in the house if there's room for one), but in styling with consideration, I make it that. Even if it's just a tiny corner.

When you're living in a shared space, assess what goes where as if you were styling any other room. Determine if there is sufficient storage. If there is sufficient shelf space. Leave room for everyone's favorite pieces. Remember that no well-styled home has just one look. Textures will bring a room together—even, maybe especially, if they don't match. You may find that a new style emerges. Make sure you're always communicating on what's working and what's not. That's the essence of sharing.

Stylish storage plus decluttering tips

The first step to keeping storage stylish is to avoid clutter.
If your house is filled to the brim with stuff, it will feel
overwhelming. Things need their place. If there is no place
for it, assess if it's something you actually need. It's worth
going through your belongings each season and deciding if
unnecessary things are taking up valuable space. Take one
room at a time and consider each item and its worth. Ask
yourself if it's useful, if it's meaningful, or if it simply makes you
happy.

We don't believe in a traditional junk drawer. It's all too
easy to throw something into it and never think about it again.
We have drawers with junk, but it's organized junk. And we like
to think it's not actually junk. Use small boxes and jars in your
drawers to organize items that get collected over time (rubber
bands, paper clips, pens, stamps, pushpins, batteries, cords)
and keep them in their designated places. We like to keep
things we use all the time or emergency items handy—a pad
of paper and pen on the counter, as well as a small attractive
metal box that sits by a door with screwdrivers, flashlights, and
matches.

As for storage, we love baskets. The wide range in price
and size are what make these the most useful storage
solution in any home. You can find them in cardboard, fabric,
metal, wood, and sea grass, in any assortment of colors and
patterns. They are amazing ways to clean up a shelf, a closet,
a side table, or a corner. They are attractive side by side or on
their own, old or new, and can be constantly repurposed for
another space or use.

In the Style chapter, we talked about multipurpose
furniture. The same goes for storage. Find a storage ottoman.
Use side tables that can hold your baskets or have drawers.
Use shelves that alternate between open shelving and having

doors. Use your furniture as is, but store things underneath for added space. You can use plastic storage boxes or roll-out drawers under beds. Slide short boxes inconspicuously under side tables and sofas. This is how we tend to store our remotes and chargers. Remember, vertical storage can offer more space and can bring height and design elements (intersperse your stylish storage with picture frames, plants, and trinkets). Going up is often easier than filling out.

Your stuff doesn't define you, but it can easily take over your life. Storage will always be a continuous battle. Be gracious with yourself for being human. Having your space feel perfect is one thing. Having it actually be perfect is something else entirely. Let's focus on feeling. ●

I've learned that people will forget
what you said, people will forget
what you did, but people will never
forget how you made them feel.

Maya Angelou

**While you want to make your home a space that caters
to your own needs and aesthetics, there is something so
special about making others feel appreciated, welcome,
and right at home when they pay you a visit—or stay a
little longer.**

From dinner parties to providing a bed for a traveling friend
in need or even renting out a spare room, being a gracious
host is an enviable attribute. But it's easy to make someone
feel welcome if your home is designed to do just that.

Find the things that bring you the most joy, and it will
inevitably feel special for your guests. Don't shy away from
sharing traditions that are unique to your household, like
homemade bread, or ice cream in your morning coffee.
As kids, we were served simple things, but when it was
presented in a special glass (like Aunt Patty's china or
Grandma Lam's antique tea set), we felt like royalty. We
will never forget how it made us feel, and the glamour of
that should be extended to guests of all ages. The simplest
traditions can almost feel sacred. Preparing for guests is
one of our favorite things to do—believe it or not—as it's
an opportunity to share some of our treasured items and
home comforts with friends, family, and even strangers.

For overnight guests, start with the bed. Make it up nicely with cozy bedding and extra pillows. Always provide an extra throw blanket for those who sleep cold. Spritz all bedding with lavender. Have a set of towels near the bed for them to use and place a chocolate on the pillow to make it feel like a vacation. Include a welcome note with some kind words and your Wi-Fi password. Set out a couple of books and magazines you think they may enjoy. If you're feeling really creative, you can add a note and map on top with a list of potential things to do and your favorite spots for a beer, a pastry, or a walk. Add a tray next to the bed with some face mist, a carafe of water and a glass, along with a dish to stash jewelry, wallets, or a watch. Keep a soft night-light as a nighttime guide in case your guest needs the bathroom, the kitchen, or just a breath of fresh air after hours.

The key to being a good host is giving your guest options for both personal and shared space, reflective time and shared time. Everyone has different needs and expectations. It's best to be clear on what you have time for and what you can offer. You are not only making room in your home, you are making room in your life, too.

Hosting can be exhausting, but we love to do it and do it often. It doesn't always involve guests staying the night. Hosting meals is just as much a labor of love. Try to loosely plan all the major aspects in advance. Prepare a space for coats and bags. Set a playlist for ambience (see Resources). Put out a cheeseboard and linen napkins. Create a DIY bar cart so your guests can feel comfortable making a cocktail or pouring themselves a glass of wine. The most successful events are those where everyone can make themselves at home. Make it easy to find utensils, a lemon, a glass, and extra salt. The meal is generally secondary because guests are there to share time with you.

Styling Advice

How to style a cheeseboard

A good cheeseboard is such an easy and stylish way to
host. It's good for parties of two and parties of twelve.
In the same way you would style a room, make sure there
is a balance of all the different elements. Layer it with
texture and color and variety. Choose a large enough
board for everything you plan on serving. Choose a range
of at least three cheeses (preslice the hard cheeses).
Add crackers, quince paste, charcuterie. Add olives and
pickles and nuts, fresh and dried fruit, fresh and pickled
vegetables. Add sardines. Add a tapenade. The beauty of
a cheeseboard is the cheeseboard. Go wild.

How to style a table

All meals should be served with care and consideration.
If you're going to put time and effort into cooking and
plating, you should certainly put the same effort into
creating a mood. How big a table is, how big plates are, and
whether a meal will be served family style or by you are all
factors to consider.

Start from the middle and then move outward. A
foliage table runner is a simple, timeless way to start.
Lay eucalyptus or olive branches down the center of the
table like a runner to create depth and an organic line.
Any greenery will really work here. If serving plates will
be on the table, consider a more traditional fabric runner
that can lay perfectly flat. Burlap and linen are attractive
choices, as well as those with geometric prints.

Centerpieces come next. You'll want to keep centerpieces
low enough that guests can see and talk to one another

across the table. If you're using foraged materials, ensure they are insect-free! We encourage using a lot of greenery. Fern cuttings in vases along with ample candlelight at different heights are a great way to add depth but not be too distracting. Try magnolia for a little color or lunaria silver dollar seedpods for sophistication.

Tying a little sprig of a fresh herb around your linen napkins and topping your plates with a stone and handwritten table card really complete the table.

True hospitality can be subtle but, when done right, it makes guests feel right at home. That's what a good host does. They spoil you seemingly effortlessly. They have considered everything from food allergies to drink preferences. They take your coat at the door, immediately point out where the bathroom is, play good music, and have plenty of snacks and refreshments. They have made the entire house smell amazing and alluring. They are keeping you well fed, laughing, and comfortable. No one can force you to get along with others, but truth be told, if your host is interesting and thoughtful and friendly, their friends probably are, too. And when it comes to the end of the night, no one wants to leave.

When you're hosting, the trick is to treat your guests like family. They are in your home. That means they are.

Table-setting tips

Do you always forget where cutlery and wine and water glasses go? Here's a quick recap:

— Forks go to the left of the plate (salad forks are to the left of the dinner fork)

— Knives (with the sharp edge facing the plate) go to the right of the plate

— Spoons go to the right of the knife

— Water glasses go above the knife

— Wineglasses go to the left of the water glass

8
Travel

Choose your corner, pick away at it carefully, intensely, and to the best of your ability, and that way you might change the world.

Charles Eames

We travel often. We're constantly on the move. So we're always looking for things that ground and connect us to what feels like home. When we rent a vacation home, we take the time to make it ours by adding wild pieces we find outside and by putting our food and snacks in bowls. When we go camping, we bring our favorite blanket, set up an outdoor cooking space, and use our everyday utensils. If we're going to be in and out of the car for a few days, we pick some flowers to put in Mason jars that live in our cup holders.

Our style follows us everywhere. You can live creatively and considerately wherever you go. You can make anywhere feel like home. And you should. It becomes a part of you.

As you continue styling your spaces, that consideration begins to follow you around. It's hard to stop, because you begin to see what a difference it makes to your day. You start to crave good style. You look for it. You start to notice what other people, or places, are doing that create a feeling or mood that you want to replicate in your own home. You start to pay attention to all your senses. To all the details.

Making a statement about who you are doesn't have to stay with where you live and work. From the pen you carry, to a custom business card holder, or your notebook filled with ideas and observations—it's a gentle reminder that consideration is worth the effort. Each time you are away from home, take something that grounds you. We happen to want our jewelry wrapped in pretty pouches and our vintage Swiss Army knives to go in our old leather travel bags. We want our things to speak to us and for us. To remind us who we are and to convey what we care about.

DQ: I choose everything I buy based on good design or sentiment or, even better, both. So when I travel, I see no reason to sacrifice those things. When I'm in a new or strange place, I enjoy using things that are exactly what I need. So while I don't consider myself to be high-maintenance, I do reach for a few considered items before leaving home. I try to plan ahead and think about what I might need for each leg of a journey. I like being prepared, not just for adventure but also for any unexpected encounter. It may even be worthy of a handwritten note—I always take extra notecards just in case.

SF: I carry my style with me. I don't do it consciously. I've been styling and photographing and generally paying attention for a very long time. I have always loved detail. I love how it makes me feel, how it makes me care more about the world, how stimulating it is. I'm constantly inspired, challenged, learning, adapting. I think the more you see the world, the more of the world you seek. And as I do this, my style evolves. The things I care about become more apparent. I carry with me the things that remind me of what I care most about. When I think about styling a space, it is no longer just about the space. It's about the people who inhabit it. I think about its purpose. It's about sharing, and cultivating, and growing. I want to take that everywhere.

When you bring objects you care about with you, you're showing you care about your things, what you use, who you are, and how things look. It is bold, confident, and important and makes a statement. Yes, we can all live simpler lives and survive on the bare minimum (well, maybe not all of us). However, that's not always the best or even most sustainable or realistic way to live. We carry our own water bottles and our favorite totes, not only because they look better, but because they create less impact on the environment when we travel—even if it's just to the city for the day.

This world is a beautiful place. It's also a beautiful mess. We can carry with us the things that we believe make it more beautiful and, in turn, create more beauty wherever we go.

Our ten travel essentials

1. **Insulated water bottle**—from hot coffee to iced tea, day or night: the ultimate simple comfort

2. **A pen, notebook, and postcard clipped inside**—for the perfect host, a new friend, or sweet reminders

3. **Turkish towel or extra-large scarf**—perfect for beach days, for nights out, and as a makeshift blanket on planes, trains, and automobiles

4. **Biodegradable wet wipes**—never underestimate a fresh face (and always dispose of these in a garbage bin)

5. **A packable tote**—for the market, unexpected souvenirs, and, of course, foraging

6. **Earplugs and an eye mask**—sound sleep is the best sleep

7. **Handkerchief**—for messes and style (tie it around your wrist or neck, use it as a pocket square, or have it loosely tucked inside a pocket)

8. **A TSA-approved keychain-size multi-tool on a clip or carabiner**—for always being prepared (even if it's just to open a bottle of beer)

9. **Zippered pouch**—for keepsakes, passports, and all things too easy to lose

10. **Attractive luggage tag**—because sometimes no matter how prepared you are, things get lost (it's also good to keep a written list of important numbers and addresses, and copies of your tickets and travel documents)

At some point in life
the world's beauty
becomes enough.

—

Toni Morrison

Conclusion

As you look around, you should start to see stories emerge from every shelf and consideration peek from every corner. Your style should start to feel intentional. Consideration and creativity are hopefully becoming dominant features of your space.

Beauty is a great igniter. To be better, try harder, look further.

As you inhabit your space and style it in such a way that reflects who you are and who you want to be, remember you, too, are ever evolving. Your home is a gathering place to nurture growth, ideas, change, and beauty. It exists to foster relationships and creativity. It's meant to nourish, replenish, protect. It is a collective of moments, stories, and artifacts.

Paying attention to what you seek, to what catches your eye, and to what makes you happy are all the steps to a fuller life. If you always remember to keep looking and keep trying, your home will undoubtedly reflect your efforts. Living a creative and considered life starts with paying attention and with caring.

When each corner of your home has been considered, it will inevitably spread into the corners of your life. At the center of making a beautiful space, style is often what is missing. As you find your style, as you take the time to consider what is missing and fill your spaces with things that are meaningful to you, we hope you find joy and gratitude for all the beauty you are bringing in. Style, like most things, comes with practice. Keep practicing. Be patient. Pay attention. *Prutsen.*

Resources

Books

Big Magic: Creative Living Beyond Fear by Elizabeth Gilbert
Cabin Porn by Steven Leckart and Zach Klein
Eames: Beautiful Details by Eames Demetrios
Foraged Flora by Louesa Roebuck and Sarah Lonsdale
In the Company of Women by Grace Bonney
Rock the Shack by S. Ehmann and S. Borges
salt. by Nayyirah Waheed
The Book of Hygge by Louisa Thomsen Brits
The Nature Fix by Florence Williams
The Selby Is in Your Place by Todd Selby
The Way She Wears It by Dallas Shaw
Upstream by Mary Oliver

Podcasts

TED Radio Hour—*What Is Beauty?* and *Slowing Down*
Hidden Brain—*You 2.0: Deep Work*
99% Invisible—*Usonia 1* and *Usonia the Beautiful*
Design Matters with Debbie Millman

Playlists

Visit Soundcloud to find our Wild Habit playlists:
soundcloud.com/wildhabit/sets

About the Authors

Sue Fan (right) is a freelance photographer, stylist, and art director who strives to live and share a meaningful life. She can often be found traipsing with her two wild dogs in different corners of the world creating or capturing beauty.

Danielle Quigley (left) is a designer and maker living with her husband, young son, and big dog in Southern California, where she is constantly working on creating a wilder and more beautiful life. She is at her best when playing outside and making pretty things.

Sue and Danielle created WILD HABIT, a lifestyle brand that takes inspiration from nature to design homeware, jewelry, and spaces with the guiding principles of respecting the environment and sharing the natural beauty of the world. Together they have created installations for corporations, restaurants, shops, studios, and homes; and have styled for the Do Lectures Wales and USA as well as private clients and events.

You can find them on Instagram:
@suefan @dquigley @wildhabit

Thanks

To the Wild—for giving us limitless inspiration and our greatest source of joy.

To all our amazing hosts who made this book come to life with their spaces or images:

Bruna and Andrew at The Barn in Tivoli, New York—for true generosity and kindness in allowing us to share your beautiful barn throughout so many of these pages (*@thebarnintivoli*).

Mimi and Richard at Made in Ghent, New York—for showing us how beauty, sustainability, and passion coexist (*@madeinghent*).

Ariele Alasko—for kinship and sharing your space, beautiful art, and inspiration (*@arielealasko*).

Christian Harder, Jeska and Dean Hearne, John David Becker, Damien Noble Andrews, and Helena Price—for your unmatched abilities to capture beauty and your willingness to share it.

Miranda West—for your guidance, voice, and wrangling.

Wilf Whitty—for your impeccable eye and unwavering patience.

The Hieatts—for exuding a life of creativity and consideration and sharing your magic with us.

Louisa Thomsen-Brits, Gaye Wolfson, Libby DeLana, and Wanda Weller—for adding such love to everything you touch, and so generously.

Anja Dunk—for being a constant source of inspiration, encouragement, and much of the reason we fell so hard for Wales and so fatefully into Do.

And the rest of our Do Family—for always feeding us, inspiring us, and teaching us to be better doers.

Sue

To those who show me every day what beauty looks like and who inspire it. You are many and I am so grateful.

To DQ—for growing my wild.

To my family—for constantly showing me selflessness and how love lives in the details.

To JB—for always pushing me, and for sharing a life that plants our feet firmly in the clouds. Our roots grow from stars.

Danielle

To Alex Karlsen—you are unwavering in your support of my wild ways. For living among the piles of sticks and stones, for giving me all the things I don't even know I need, and for your steadfast patience, insight, and encouragement.

To Sue Fan—for giving me a friendship, a partnership, and a co-authorship that is unmatched in its devotion, integrity, and thoughtfulness. I'll never tire of us playing outside and making pretty things together.

To Kim and Dan Quigley, and Nicole Finnegan—for continually seeking beauty in the smallest of things and for never taking the big things for granted.

Books in the series:

A percentage of royalties from each copy sold will go to the DO Lectures, a workshop series for sharing ideas and inspiring action.

For more in the DO Books series, visit **www.chroniclebooks.com**.

To learn more about DO Lectures, visit **www.thedolectures.com**.